THIS BOOK BELONGS TO:

This book is dedicated to
Gabriel Burgess, Malachi Wilson,
Ashton Bodiford, and Cullen Gormley
who were all kept out of school for
wearing their hair in their own family
or culturally traditional style.

And for Kaleo, my grandson,
who inspires me daily with his
curiosity, perceptiveness, and wisdom.

See if you can count how many times you can find Kaleo's picture in this book. Answer on page 30.

Long Hair Don't Care © 2016 Jill Guerra

First Edition
Printed in the U.S.

Summary: A poem picture book about boys and men with long hair.

ISBN: 978-0-692-54026-8
Library of Congress Control Number: 2016900792

Design by Joy Liu-Trujillo for Swash Design Studio

For more information about this book, please visit: **thelovecurriculum.com**

Long Hair Don't Care

A POEM ABOUT BOYS WITH LONG HAIR

BY JILL GUERRA

Keep Shining Your Light!

Jill Guerra ♡

Boys with long hair everywhere in sight!

Long-haired boys everywhere,

Big boys, little boys, boys with hair!

Long hair playing sports with balls.

Long-haired boys big and small.

Long hair up on days that are hotter.

Long hair kisses on the cheek.

Long hair is beautiful and unique.

Long hair eating delicious food.

Long hair in a silly mood.

13

Long hair working answers out.

Long-haired boys love their pets.

Long-haired boys sometimes get upset.

Long hair cuddling on Daddy's lap.

18

Long hair needing a nice long nap.

Long hair sharing loving hearts.

25

Long hair, long hair, for anyone!

About the Author

Jill Guerra has been teaching in the Oakland public schools for twelve years. She is a witness to the lack of diversity among books for children and knows that children need to see themselves in their own shining light. For years, she has collected every picture and chapter book she could find that exemplifies diversity in all its forms. She feels very lucky that the Bay Area, where she raised her children, currently teaches and where her own long-haired grandson attends school, is open-minded and embraces the beauty of difference. Jill hopes to one day spend full days teaching Mindfulness to youth and writing children's books. This is her first attempt at the latter. For more information, visit: **thelovecurriculum.com**.

(Above: Author taking down her grandson's hair.)

Acknowledgements

Achievements are never attained in isolation, so I must acknowledge several people. First, I want to express my deepest gratitude to all of the individuals and families that contributed photographs. Your images are so beautiful and I am grateful! Thank you to Joy Liu-Trujillo because this book wouldn't be what it is without you. Mil gracias to Maya Christina Gonzalez for all of the lessons on writing, art, and letting the creativity come through. Thank you Aya de León for the inspiration and the talk; it helped more than you know. My babies, Sophia and Antonino, thank you for helping me grow. Gratitude to my mama, Elsa, for the unconditional love and support... and to my love and life partner, Chris, for supporting me in anything and everything I do. LOVE.

Photo Credits

All images used with permission.
Photo of Julio Remelexo on page 2 by Raquel Castillo.
Wedding photographs on pages 10, 22, 23, and 27 by Bethanie Hines (bethaniehines.com).
Wedding photograph on page 13 by Andria Lo (andrialo.com).
Photo of Johnny Turfinc Lopez on page 21 provided by Kyle Davidson of Intwovision.

Kaleo's image can be found on the following pages: Dedication, 2, 6, 7, 8, 9, 10, 11, 12 (two times), 14, 17, 19, 22, 24, 25, 27, and 29. *18 times!*

Made in the USA
San Bernardino, CA
22 November 2016